41 REASONS I'M STAYING IN

To all the introverts
I've met
and
May never meet

wm An Imprint of WILLIAM MORROW
MORROW
GIFT

41

REASONS I'M STAYING IN

A Celebration of Introverts

Hallie Heald

" I believe I know the only cure,
which is to make one's center
of life inside of one's self,
not selfishly, or excludingly,
but with a kind of unassailable
serenity-to decorate one's
inner house so richly
that one is content there,
glad to welcome any one
who wants to come
but happy all the same
when one is inevitably alone."

- Edith Wharton

41 REASONS I'M STAYING IN

WELCOME

EAT croissants
SMOKE ciggs   WEar Pearls
Repeat

AUDREY HEPBURN

Chicken Noodle SOUP

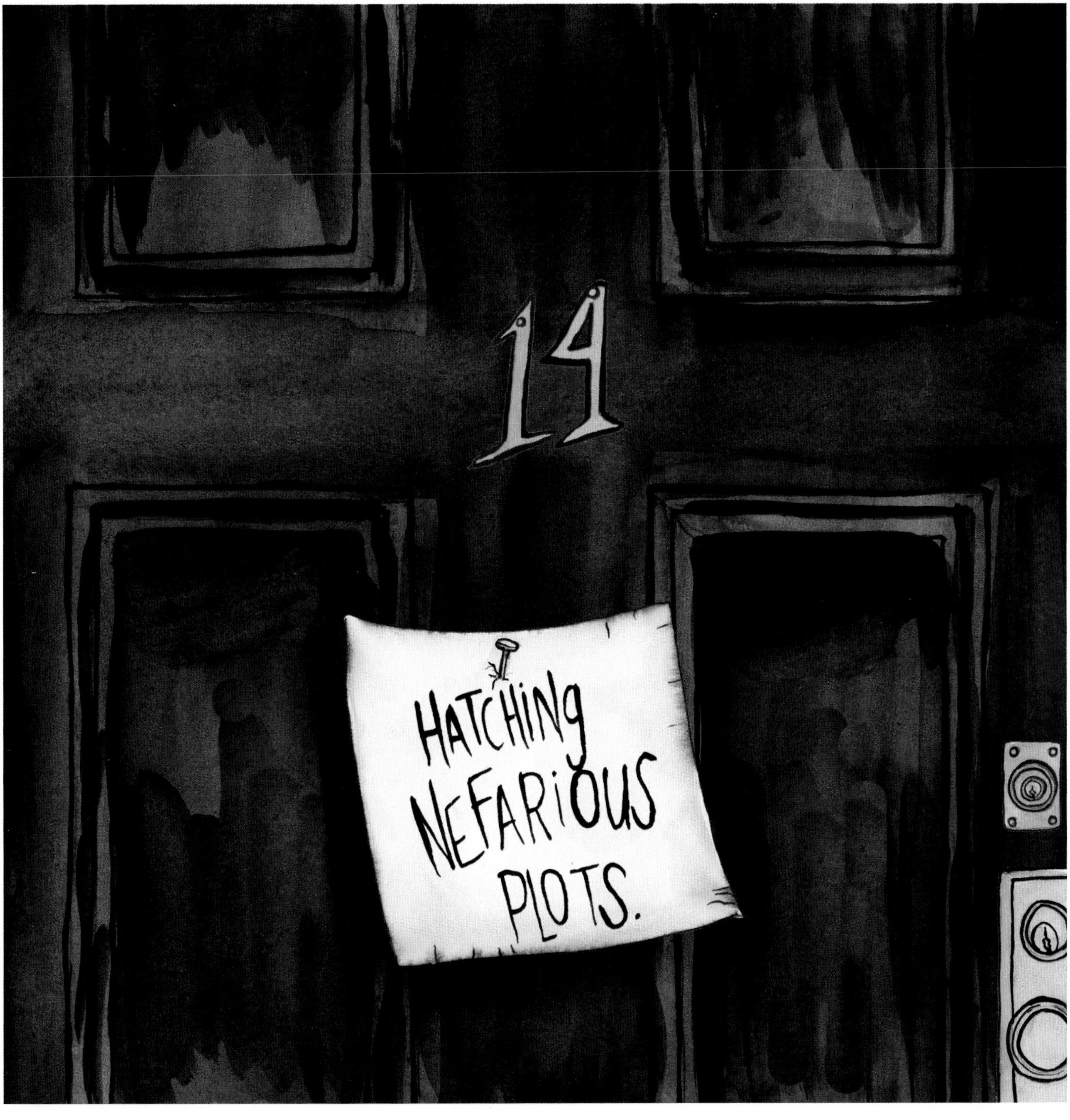
14
HATCHING NEFARIOUS PLOTS.

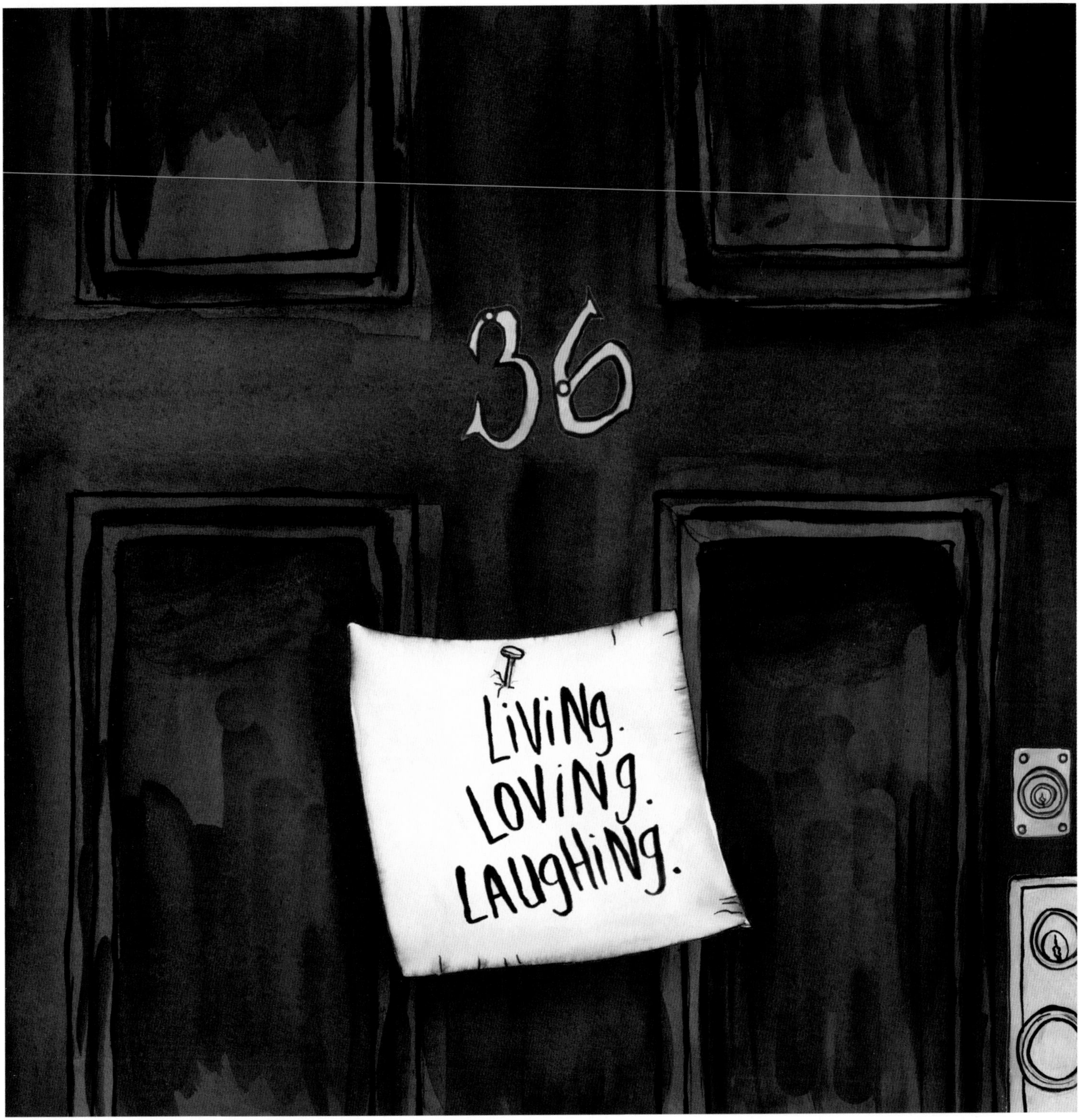
36
LIVING.
LOVING.
LAUGHING.

A special thanks to...

Sara Reinis for her support and consultation.

My editor, Emma Brodie, for believing in my ideas and guiding me through the creation of this book.

The dream team at William Morrow: Liate Stehlik, Lynn Grady, Cassie Jones, Susan Kosko, Andrea Molitor, Leah Carlson-Stanisic, Mumtaz Mustafa, Maria Silva, and Tavia Kowalchuk.

My friends (introverted and extroverted), for their encouragement along the way.

My family: Charlie, Lucy Wu, Bella, Lee Lee, Louisa, Anders, Hamilton, Frances, Mom, and dad, for the calls, voicemails, texts, videos, memes, snail-mail, visits, hugs, advice, laughter, dance parties, movie nights, posing for book characters, and keeping me sane. Without your love this book would not exist.

My agent, Joy, for standing by me and teaching me to see the value in my work.

And lastly, to my room.

Hallie Heald is a freelance book illustrator and portrait painter in New York. 41 Reasons I'm Staying In, is her first book to write and second to illustrate. Heald was born a lone introvert in a family of nine kids, and spent her days painting and listening to audiobooks, years later she's doing the same thing in a different bedroom. The idea for this book was inspired by Season 1 episode 4 of Seinfeld, titled "Male Unbonding" in which Jerry and Elaine invent excuses to avoid an unwanted evening out: jury duty, choir practice, etc. Her work can also be found in The Women Who Made New York and has been featured in the New York Times, NY Mag, The Cut, Village Voice, Elle, and Brain Pickings.

HarperCollins books may be purchased for educational, business, or sales promotional use. For information, please email the Special Markets Department at SPsales@harpercollins.com.

FIRST EDITION

Designed by Leah Carlson-Stanisic

Library of Congress Cataloging-in-Publication Data has been applied for.

ISBN 978-0-06-274989-5
19 20 21 22 23 SC 10 9 8 7 6 5 4 3 2 1